FUNNY POEMS

FUNNY POEMS

edited by
Deborah Manley

Illustrated by Gillian Chapman

A DRAGON BOOK

GRANADA
London Toronto Sydney New York

Published by Granada Publishing Limited in 1982

ISBN 0 583 30503 2

Copyright © in this edition Deborah Manley

Granada Publishing Limited
Frogmore, St Albans, Herts AL2 2NF
and
36 Golden Square, London W1R 4AH
866 United Nations Plaza, New York, NY 10017, USA
117 York Street, Sydney, NSW 2000, Australia
100 Skyway Avenue, Rexdale, Ontario, M9W 3A6, Canada
61 Beach Road, Auckland, New Zealand

Printed and bound in Great Britain by
Cox and Wyman Ltd, Reading

Set in Goudy

This book is for Catherine and James

Acknowledgements

My *name is* is reprinted by kind permission of Curtis Brown Ltd on behalf of Pauline Clarke; *I've had this shirt* and *My dad's thumb* are reprinted by kind permission of Michael Rosen and André Deutsch Ltd from *Mind your own business*; *My father* and *Other folk's folks* are reprinted by permission of Faber and Faber Ltd from *Meet my folks* by Ted Hughes; *Daddy fell into the pond* by Alfred Noyes is reprinted by permission of Blackwood and Sons Ltd; *Appreciation* by Harry Graham is reprinted by permission of Edward Arnold Ltd; *Extremely naughty children* from *Green Outside* by Elizabeth Godley, copyright 1932 (renewed 1960 by Elizabeth Godley) is reprinted by permission of Viking Penguin Inc; *Johnnie Crack and Flossie Snail* is reprinted by permission of the Trustees for the copyright for the late Dylan Thomas and J. M. Dent and Sons Ltd from *Under Milkwood*; *George's pet* by Margaret Mahy is reprinted by permission of J. M. Dent and Sons Ltd from *Nonstop Nonsense*; *The vulture* and *The elephant* by Hilaire Belloc are reprinted by permission of Duckworth and Co Ltd; *Miss T* is reprinted by permission of the Literary Trustees of Walter de la Mare and the Society of Authors as their representative; *The Wendigo*, *A caution to everybody* and *The sniffle* are reprinted from *Verses from 1929 on* by Ogden Nash by perission of the Estate of Ogden Nash and Little, Brown and Co. *The Wendigo* and *A caution to everybody* copyright 1953 by Ogden Nash. *The sniffle*, copyright 1941 by The Curtis Publishing Co, first appeared in *Ladies Home Journal*; *Colonel Fazackerley* is printed by permission of Charles Causley and Macmillan from *Figgie Hobbin*; *The old sailor* is reprinted by permission of the Estate of A. A. Milne and Methuen Children's Books and MacClelland and Stewart from *Now we are six*; *The lesson* is reprinted by permission of Roger McGough and Jonathan Cape Ltd from *In the Classroom*; *The Snitterjipe* and *The Hippocrump* are reprinted by permission of William Heinemann Ltd; *The serpent* is reprinted by permission of Faber and Faber Ltd and Doubleday and Co Inc, copyright 1950 from *The Collected Poems of Theodore Roethke*; *The centipede's song* is reprinted by permission or Roald Dahl, George Allen and Unwin Ltd and Alfred Knopf Random House Inc from *James and the giant peach* by Roald Dahl; *silly old baboon* is reprinted by permission of Spike Milligan and Dobson Books Ltd from *A book of Milliganimals* by Spike Milligan; *The rabbit* and *The shark* are reprinted by permission of Edward Colman, Literary Executor of Lord Alfred Douglas and Batsford Ltd from *Tails with a twist: Animal nonsense verse*; *Hard Cheese* is reprinted by kind permission of G. Summerfield; *The computer's first Christmas* is reprinted by permission of Edinburgh University Press from *The Second Life*.

Despite every effort the editor and publishers have been unable to trace the holders of copyright in: *The young fellow* by Gelett Burgess, *The purple cow* by Carolyn Wells, *Not so gorgeous* and *The sink song* by J. A. Lindon, *The sleeping bag* by H. G. Ponting, *The elephant* and *The giraffe* by John Joy Bell, *The pessimist* by Benjamin Franklin King, *The camel's complaint* by Charles E. Carryl.

My name is . . .

My name is Sluggery-wuggery
My name is Worms-for-tea
My name is Swallow-the-table-leg
My name is Drink-the-Sea.
My name is I-eat-saucepans
My name is I-like-snails
My name is Grand-piano-George
My name is I-ride-whales.

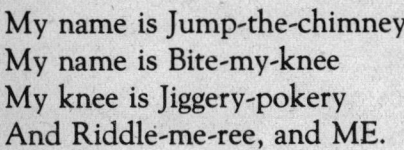

My name is Jump-the-chimney
My name is Bite-my-knee
My knee is Jiggery-pokery
And Riddle-me-ree, and ME.

PAULINE CLARKE

A song about myself

There was a naughty boy,
    A naughty boy was he,
He would not stop at home,
    He could not quiet be –
        He took
        In his knapsack
        A book
        Full of vowels
        And a shirt
        With some towels –

A slight cap
For a night-cap –
A hair brush,
Comb ditto,
New stockings,
For old ones
Would split O!
This knapsack
Tight at's back
He riveted close
And followed his nose
To the North,
To the North,
And followed his nose
To the North.

There was a naughty boy,
And a naughty boy was he,
He ran away to Scotland
The people for to see –
There he found
That the ground
Was as hard,
That a yard
Was as long,
That a song
Was as merry,
That a cherry
Was as red,
That lead
Was as weighty,

8

That fourscore
Was as eighty,
That a door
Was as wooden
As in England –
So he stood in his shoes
And he wondered,
He wondered,
He stood in his shoes
And he wondered.

JOHN KEATS

It ain't gonna rain no more

It ain't gonna rain no more, no more,
It ain't gonna rain no more;
So how in the heck can I wash my neck
If it ain't gonna rain no more?

UNKNOWN

What animals drop from the clouds?
The rain, dear.

9

I've had this shirt

I've had this shirt
that's covered in dirt
for years and years and years.

It used to be red
but I wore it in bed
and it went grey
cos I wore it all day
for years and years and years.

The arms fell off
in the Monday wash
and you can see my vest
through the holes in the chest
for years and years and years.

As my shirt falls apart
I'll keep the bits
in a biscuit tin
on the mantelpiece
for years and years and years.

MICHAEL ROSEN

Where does Tarzan buy his clothes?
At jungle sales.

My father

Some fathers work at the office, others work at the
    store,
Some operate great cranes and build up sky-
    scrapers galore,
Some work in canning factories counting green
    peas into cans,
Some drive all night in huge and thundering
    removal vans.

    But mine has the strangest job of the lot.
    My Father's the Chief Inspector of – What?
    O don't tell the mice, don't tell the moles,
    My Father's the Chief Inspector of HOLES.

It's a work of the highest importance because you
    never know
What's in a hole, what fearful thing is creeping
    from below.
Perhaps it's a hole to the ocean and will soon gush
    water in tons,
Or maybe it leads to a vast cave full of gold and
    skeletons.

    Though a hole might seem to have nothing but
        dirt in,
    Somebody's simply got to make certain.
    Caves in the mountain, clefts in the wall,
    My father has to inspect them all.

That crack in the road looks harmless. My Father
 knows it's not.
The world may be breaking into two and starting at
 that spot.
Or maybe the world is a great egg, and we live on
 the shell,
And it's just beginning to split and hatch: you
 simply cannot tell.

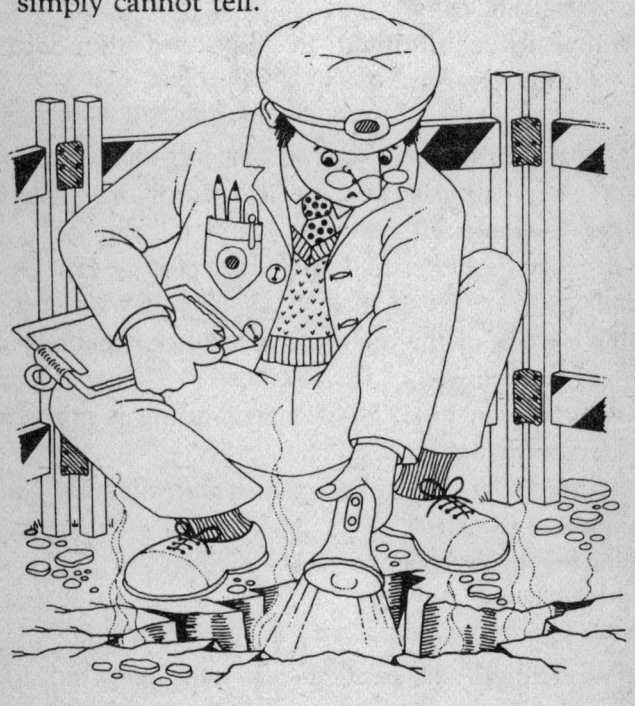

If you see a crack, run to the phone, run;
My Father will know just what's to be done.
A rumbling hole, a silent hole,
My father will soon have it under control.

Keeping a check on all these holes he hurries from
    morning to night.
There might be sounds of marching in one, or an
    eye shining bright.
A tentacle came groping from a hole that belonged
    to a mouse,
A floor collapsed and Chinamen swarmed up into
    the house.
        A Hole's an unpredictable thing –
        Nobody knows what a Hole might bring.
        Caves in the mountain, clefts in the wall,
        My father has to inspect them all!

                                        TED HUGHES

*What do you get when you cross an elephant and a
kangaroo?*

Great big holes all over Australia.

Not so gorgeous

Dorothy's drawers are creamy gauze;
    Lil's are long and slack;
Tonia's tights are crocheted whites;
    Jennifer Jane's are black.

Betty's bloomers are slaty grey,
    And she tucks her skirt inside;
Polly's are pink– since yesterday –
    I think she's had them dyed.

Sarah's silks were awf'ly dear –
    The best her mum could get;
And (may I whisper it in your ear?)
    Nancy's knickers are wet!

Sue's are blue, and Prue's are too,
    And little Pam's are sweet;
While naughty Meg has lost a leg,
    And Tilly has torn her seat.

Swanky Maisie's are trimmed with daisies
    And patched with coloured stuffs;
But those on Milly look awful silly –
    They sort of flap their cuffs!

Jill's have frills, and Pat's are plain,
    With a button in case they fall;
And (may I whisper once again?)
    I haven't a pair at all!

J.A. LINDON

*What is black and sticky and comes out of the ground
shouting, 'Knickers, knickers!'*
Crude oil.

My dad's thumb

My dad's thumb
can stick pins in wood
without flinching –
it can crush family-size matchboxes
in one stroke
and lever off jam-jar lids without piercing
at the pierce here sign.

If it wanted
it could be a bath-plug
or a paint-scraper
a keyhole cover or a tap-tightener.

It's already a great nutcracker
and if it dressed up
it could easily pass
as a broad bean or a big toe.

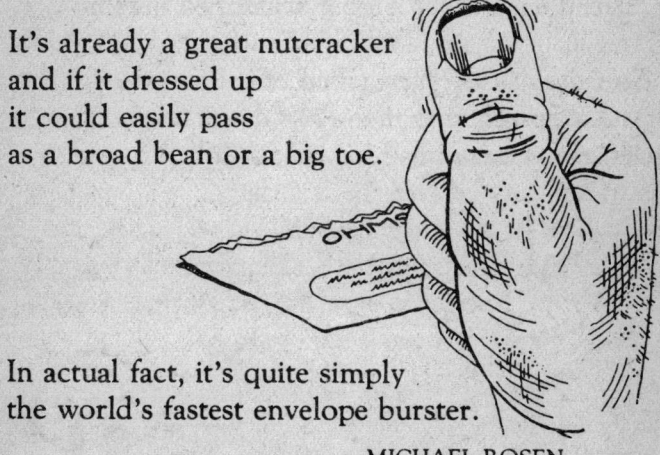

In actual fact, it's quite simply
the world's fastest envelope burster.

MICHAEL ROSEN

What did the big firework say to the small firework?

My pop is bigger than yours.

Daddy fell into the pond

Everyone grumbled. The sky was grey.
We had nothing to do and nothing to say.
We were nearing the end of a dismal day.
And there seemed to be nothing beyond,
  Then
      Daddy fell into the pond!

And everyone's face grew merry and bright,
And Timothy danced for sheer delight.
'Give me the camera, quick, oh quick!
He's crawling out of the duckweed!' Click!

Then the gardener suddenly slapped his knee,
And doubled up, shaking silently,
And the ducks all quacked as if they were daft,
And it sounded as if the old drake laughed.
Oh, there wasn't a thing that didn't respond
  When
      Daddy fell into the pond!

ALFRED NOYES

What is a certain way to get a wild duck?
Buy a tame one and annoy it.

You are old, Father William

'You are old, Father William,' the young man said,
  'And your hair has become very white;
And yet you incessantly stand on your head –
  Do you think, at your age, it is right?'

'In my youth,' Father William replied to his son,
  'I feared it might injure the brain;
But, now that I'm perfectly sure I have none,
  Why, I do it again and again.'

'You are old,' said the youth, 'as I mentioned
    before,
  And have grown most uncommonly fat;
Yet you turned a back-somersault in at the door –
  Pray, what is the reason of that?'

'In my youth,' said the sage, as he shook his grey
    locks,
  'I kept all my limbs very supple
By the use of this ointment – one shilling the box –
  Allow me to sell you a couple?'

'You are old,' said the youth, 'and your jaws are too
    weak
  For anything tougher than suet;
Yet you finished the goose, with the bones and the
    beak –
  Pray, how did you manage to do it?'

'In my youth,' said his father, 'I took to the law,
   And argued each case with my wife;
And the muscular strength, which it gave to my
   jaw,
   Has lasted the rest of my life.'

'You are old,' said the youth, 'one would hardly
   suppose
   That your eye was as steady as ever;
Yet you balanced an eel on the end of your nose –
   What made you so awfully clever?'

'I have answered three questions, and that is
   enough,'
   Said his father; 'don't give yourself airs!
Do you think I can listen all day to such stuff?
   Be off, or I'll kick you down stairs!'

LEWIS CARROLL

Appreciation

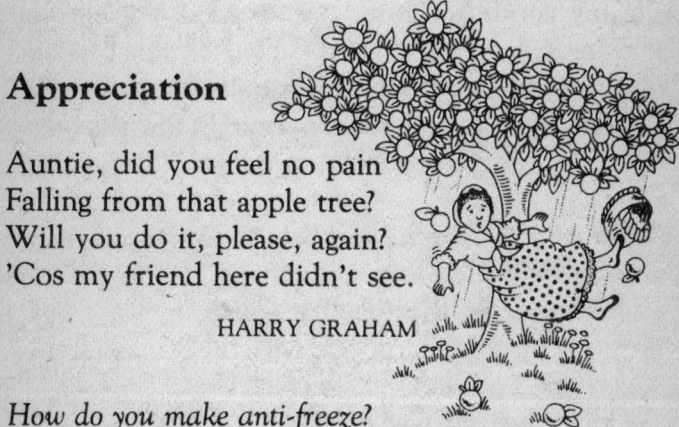

Auntie, did you feel no pain
Falling from that apple tree?
Will you do it, please, again?
'Cos my friend here didn't see.

HARRY GRAHAM

How do you make anti-freeze?
Hide her nightie.

18

My aunt

My aunt she died a month ago
    And left me all her riches –
A feather-bed, a wooden leg,
    And a pair of calico britches.
A coffee-pot without a spout,
    A mug without a handle,
A 'baccy box without a lid,
    And half a farthing candle.

UNKNOWN

Dahn the plug-'ole

A muvver was barfin' 'er biby one night,
The youngest of ten and a tiny young mite,
The muvver was pore and the biby was thin,
Only a skellington covered in skin;
The muvver turned rahnd for the soap orf the rack,
She was but a moment, but when she turned back,
The biby was gorn; and in anguish she cried,
'Oh, where is my biby?' The angels replied:
'Your biby 'as fell dahn the plug-'ole,
Your biby 'as gorn dahn the plug;
The pore little thing was so skinny and thin
'E oughter been barfed in a jug;
Your biby is perfeckly 'appy,
'E don't need a barf any more,
Your biby 'as fell dahn the plug-'ole,
Not lorst, but gorn before.'

UNKNOWN

19

How to treat grandma

When grandma visits you, my dears,
  Be good as you can be;
Don't put hot waffles in her ears,
  Or beetles in her tea.

Don't sew a pattern on her cheek
  With worsted or with silk;
Don't call her naughty names in Greek,
  Or spray her face with milk.

Don't drive a staple in her foot,
  Don't stick pins in her head;
And, oh, I beg you, do not put
  Live embers in her bed.
  These things are not considered kind;
  They worry her, and tease –
Such cruelty is not refined
  It always fails to please.

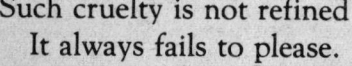

Be good to grandma, little chaps,
  Whatever else you do;
And then she'll grow to be – perhaps –
  More tolerant of you.

UNKNOWN

Extremely naughty children

By far
The naughtiest
Children
I know
Are Jasper
Geranium
James
And Jo.

They live
In a house
On the Hill
Of Kidd,
And what
In the world
Do you think
They did?

They asked
Their uncles
And aunts
To tea,
And shouted
In loud
Rude voices:
'We

Are tired
Of scoldings
And sendings
To bed:
Now
The grown-ups
Shall be
Punished instead.'

They said:
'Auntie Em,
You didn't
Say "Thank you!" '
They said:
'Uncle Robert,
We're going
To spank you!'

They pulled
The beard
Of Sir Henry
Dorner
And put him
To stand
In disgrace
In the corner.

They scolded
Aunt B.,
They punished
Aunt Jane;
They slapped
Aunt Louisa
Again
And again.

They said
'Naughty boy!'
To their
Uncle
Fred,
And boxed
His ears
And sent him
To bed.

Do you think
Aunts Em
And Loo
And B.,
And Sir
Henry
Dorner
(K.C.B.),

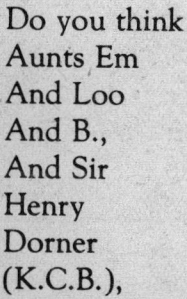

And the elderly
Uncles
And kind
Aunt Jane
Will go
To tea
With the children
Again?

ELIZABETH GODLEY

'Mother, what's a werewolf?'
'Quiet, son, and comb your face.'

Johnnie Crack and Flossie Snail

Johnnie Crack and Flossie Snail
Kept their baby in a milking pail
Flossie Snail and Johnnie Crack
One would pull it out and one would put it back

O it's my turn now said Flossie Snail
To take the baby from the milking pail
And it's my turn now said Johnnie Crack
To smack it on the head and put it back

Johnnie Crack and Flossie Snail
Kept their baby in a milking pail
One would put it back and one would pull it out
And all it had to drink was ale and stout
For Johnnie Crack and Flossie Snail
Always used to say that stout and ale
Was *good* for a baby in a milking pail.

DYLAN THOMAS

What is the hardest part of milking a mouse?
Getting the bucket under it.

George's pet

When George and his gorilla
Go bounding down the street,
They get respectful nods and smiles
From neighbours that they meet.

If George had owned a puppy dog,
Or else a kitty-cat,
His neighbours wouldn't notice him
With courtesy like that.

MARGARET MAHY

*What's white and fluffy and beats its chest in a cake
shop?*

A meringue-utang.

Other folk's folks

I've heard so much about other folk's folks,
How somebody's Uncle told such jokes
The cat split laughing and had to be stitched,
How somebody's Aunt got so bewitched
She fried the kettle and washed the water
And spanked a letter and posted her daughter.
Other folk's folks get so well known,
And nobody knows about my own.

TED HUGHES

The sleeping-bag

On the outside grows the furside, on the inside
   grows the skinside;
So the furside is the outside, and the skinside is the
   inside.
As the skinside is the inside, and the furside is the
   outside;
One 'side' likes the skinside inside, and the furside
   on the outside.
Others like the skinside outside, and the furside
   on the inside;
As the skinside is the hardside, and the furside is
   the soft side.
If you turn the skinside outside, thinking you will
   side with that 'side',
Then the soft side, furside's inside, which some
   argue is the wrong side.
If you turn the furside outside, as you say it grows
   on that side;
Then your outside's next the skinside, which for
   comfort's not the right side:
For the skinside is the cold side, and your outside's
   not your warm side;
And two cold sides coming side by side are
   not right sides one 'side' decides.
If you decide to side with that 'side', turn the
   outside, furside, inside;
Then, the hard side, cold side, skinside's, beyond
   all question, inside outside.

H. G. PONTING

Through the teeth

Through the teeth
And past the gums
Look out stomach,
Here is comes!

TRADITIONAL AMERICAN

Mix a pancake

Mix a pancake,
Stir a pancake,
      Pop it in the pan;

Fry the pancake,
Toss the pancake –
      Catch it if you can.

CHRISTINA ROSSETTI

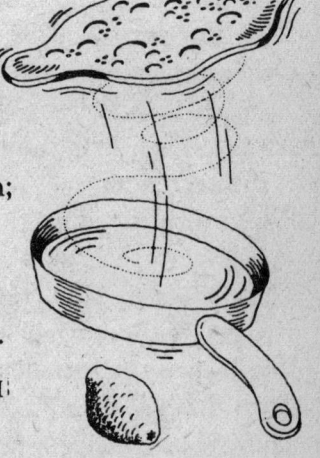

What did the astronaut see in the frying pan?
An unidentified frying object.

What's yellow inside and green outside?
A banana disguised as a cucumber.

What do cannibals play at parties?
Swallow my leader.

The vulture

The Vulture eats between his meals,
And that's the reason why
He very, very rarely feels
As well as you and I.
His eye is dull, his head is bald,
His neck is growing thinner.
Oh! what a lesson for us all
To only eat at dinner!

HILAIRE BELLOC

A puzzle

The man in the wilderness asked of me
'How many strawberries grow in the sea?'
I answered him as I thought good,
'As many red herrings as grow in the wood.'

UNKNOWN

The pelican

What a wonderful beast is the Pelican!
Whose bill can hold more than his belly can
    He can take in his beak
    Enough food for a week –
I'm damned if I know how the hell he can.

UNKNOWN

Miss T.

It's a very odd thing –
   As odd as can be –
That whatever Miss T. eats
   Turn into Miss T.;
Porridge and apples,
   Mince, muffins, and mutton,
Jam, junket, jumbles –
   Not a rap, not a button
It matters; the moment
   They're out of her plate,
Though shared by Miss Butcher
   And sour Mr Bate;
Tiny and cheerful,
   And neat as can be,
Whatever Miss T. eats
   Turns into Miss T.

WALTER DE LA MARE

The yarn of the 'Nancy Bell'

'Twas on the shores that round our coast
  From Deal to Ramsgate span,
That I found alone on a piece of stone
  An elderly naval man.

His hair was weedy, his beard was long,
  And weedy and long was he,
And I heard this wight on the shore recite,
  In a singular minor key:

'Oh, I am a cook and a captain bold,
  And the mate of the *Nancy* brig,
And a bo'sun tight, and a midshipmite,
  And the crew of the captain's gig.'

And he shook his fists and he tore his hair,
  Till I really felt afraid.
For I couldn't help thinking the man had been
    drinking,
  And so I simply said:

'Oh, elderly man, it's little I know
  Of the duties of men of the sea,
And I'll eat my hand if I understand
  How you can possibly be

At once a cook, and a captain bold,
  And the mate of the *Nancy* brig,
And a bo'sun tight and a midshipmite,
  And the crew of the captain's gig.'

Then he gave a hitch to his trousers, which
    Is a trick all seamen larn,
And having got rid of a thumping quid,
    He spun this painful yarn:

'Twas in the good ship, *Nancy Bell*,
    That we sailed to the Indian Sea,
And there on a reef we come to grief,
    Which has often occurred to me.

And pretty nigh all o' the crew was drowned
    (There was seventy-seven o'soul)
And only ten of the *Nancy's* men
    Said 'Here!' to the muster roll.

There was me and the cook and the captain bold,
   And the mate of the *Nancy* brig,
And the bo'sun tight and a midshipmite,
   And the crew of the captain's gig.

For a month we'd neither wittles nor drink,
   Till a-hungry we did feel,
So we drawed a lot, and accordin' shot
   The captain for our meal.

The next lot fell to the *Nancy's* mate,
   And a delicate dish he made;
Then our appetite with the midshipmite
   We seven survivors stayed.

And then we murdered the bo'sun tight,
   And he much resembled pig;
Then we wittled free, did the cook and me,
   On the crew of the captain's gig.

Then only the cook and me was left,
   And the delicate question, 'Which
Of us two goes to the kettle?' arose,
   And we argued it out as sich.

For I loved that cook as a brother, I did,
   And the cook he worshipped me;
But we'd both be blowed if we'd either be stowed
   In the other chap's hold, you see.

"I'll be eat if you dines off me," says Tom,
    "Yes, that," says I, "you'll be"—
"I'm boiled if I die, my friend," quoth I,
    And "exactly so," quoth he.

Says he, "Dear James, to murder me
    Were a foolish thing to do,
For don't you see that you can't cook *me*,
    While I can – and will – cook *you*!"

So he boils the water, and takes the salt
    And the pepper in portions true
(Which he never forgot) and some chopped shalot
    And some sage and parsley too.

"Come here," says he, with a proper pride,
    Which his smiling features tell,
"'Twill soothing be if I let you see,
    How extremely nice you'll smell."

And he stirred it round and round and round,
    And he sniffed at the foaming froth:
When I ups with his heels, and smothers his squeals
    In the scum of the boiling broth.

And I eat that cook in a week or less,
    And – as I eating be
The last of his chops, why I almost drops,
    For a vessel in sight I see.

And I never grieve, and I never smile,
　And I never larf nor play,
But I sit and croak, and a single joke
　I have – which is to say:

Oh, I am a cook and a captain bold,
　And the mate of the *Nancy* brig,
And a bo'sun tight, and a midshipmite,
　And the crew of the captain's gig!'

W. S. GILBERT

What do get if you cross the Atlantic with the Titanic?
Halfway.

Salt, mustard, vinegar, pepper

Salt, Mustard, Vinegar, Pepper,
French almond rock,
Bread and butter for your supper
That's all mother's got.
Fish and chips and coca cola,
Put them in a pan,
Irish stew and ice cream soda,
We'll eat all we can.

Salt, Mustard, Vinegar, Pepper,
French almond rock,
Bread and butter for your supper
That's all mother's got.
Eggs and bacon, salted herring,
Put them in a pot,
Pickled onions, apple pudding,
We will eat the lot.

Salt, Mustard, Vinegar, Pepper,
Pig's head and trout,
Bread and butter for your supper
OUT spells out.

TRADITIONAL

What stays hot when you put it in the refrigerator?
Mustard.

What begins with T ends with T and has T in it?
A teapot.

The real history of the apple-pie

A apple-pie, B bit it,
C cut it, D dealt it,
E ate it, F fought for it,
G got it, H had it,
I iced it, J joked about it,
K kept it, L longed for it,
M mourned for it,
N nodded at it,
O opened it, P peeped in it,
Q quartered it, R ran for it,
S stole it, T took it,
U upset it, V viewed it,
W wanted it, X expected it,
Y yearned for it, Z had a zest for it;
And when they came to ampersand
They all desired a piece in hand.

At last they every one agreed
Upon the apple-pie to feed;
But as there seemed to be so many
Those who were last might not have any
Unless some method could be thought out
To stop their squabbles being fought out.
They all agreed to stand in order
Around the apple-pie's fine border,
Take turn as they in school-book stand.
From great A down to ampersand,
In equal parts the pie dividing,
A fair plan they were all deciding,

Says A, give me a good large slice,
Says B, a little bit, but nice,
Says C, cut me a piece of crust,
Take it, says D, it's dry as dust,
Says E, I'll eat it fast, I will,
Says F, I vow I'll have my fill,
Says G, give it me good and great,
Says H, a little bit I hate,
Says I, its ice I must request,
Says J, the juice I love the best,
Says K, let's keep it up above,
Says L, the border's what I love,
Says M, it makes your teeth to chatter,
N said, it's nice, there's nought the matter,
O others' plates with grief surveyed,
P for a large piece begged and prayed,
Q quarrelled for the topmost slice,
R rubbed his hands and said 'it's nice,'
S silent sat, and simply looked,
T thought, and said, it's nicely cooked,
U understood the fruit was cherry,
V vanished when they all got merry,
W wished there'd been a quince in,
X here explained he'd need convincing,
Y said, I'll eat, and yield to none,
Z, like a zany, said he'd done,
While ampersand purloined the dish,
And for another pie did wish.

UNKNOWN

The elephant

Aunt Mary is my aunt,
    She took me to the Zoo.
She offered to the Elephant
    One bun – it wanted two.

Aunt Mary had a hat
    All cherries on her head.
The beast thought, 'Buns are good, but that
    Will do quite well instead.'

The creature smiled serene,
    And made a little bow . . .
Aunt Mary's never, never seen
    Her hat from then till now.

Aunt Mary danced a jig,
    And wept till she was blind,
And screamed, 'You bad, old ugly pig!'
    But, it didn't seem to mind.

JOHN JOY BELL

Why did the elephant paint his toenails red?

So he wouldn't be noticed when he climbed up the cherry tree.

39

If you should meet a crocodile

If you should meet a crocodile
Don't take a stick and poke him;
Ignore the welcome in his smile,
Be careful not to stroke him.
For as he sleeps upon the Nile,
He thinner gets and thinner;
And where'er you meet a crocodile
He's ready for his dinner.

UNKNOWN

Would you rather a crocodile attacked you or an elephant?

I'd rather he attacked the elephant.

An oyster met an oyster

An oyster met an oyster
    And they were oysters two;
Two oysters met two oysters,
    And they were oysters too;
Four oysters met a pint of milk,
And they were oyster stew.

UNKNOWN

A noisy noise annoys an oyster.

The Wendigo*

The Wendigo,
The Wendigo!
Its eyes are ice and indigo!
Its blood is rank and yellowish!
Its voice is hoarse and bellowish!
Its tentacles are slithery,
And scummy,
Slimy,
Leathery!
Its lips are hungry blubbery,
And smacky,
Sucky,
Rubbery!
The Wendigo,
The Wendigo!
I saw it just a friend ago!
Last night it lurked in Canada;
Tonight, on your veranada!
As you are lolling hammockwise
It contemplates you stomachwise.
You loll,
It contemplates,
It lollops.
The rest is merely gulps and gollops.

OGDEN NASH

Wendigo: In the mythology of the Northern Algonquin Indians,
an evil spirit; one of a fabulous tribe of cannibals. (Webster's
Unabridged Dictionary.)

Peas

I eat my peas with honey,
I've done it all my life;
It makes the peas taste funny,
But it keeps them on the knife.

UNKNOWN

Sink song

Scouring out the porridge pot,
Round and round and round!

Out with all the scraith and scoopery,
Lift the eely ooly droopery,
Chase the glubbery slubbery gloopery
Round and round and round!

Out with all the doleful dithery,
Ladle out the slimy slithery,
Hunt and catch the hithery thithery,
Round and round and round.

Out with all the obbly gubbly,
On the stove it burns so bubbly,
Use the spoon and use it doubly,
Round and round and round.

J. A. LINDON

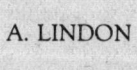

Ladles and jellyspoons

Ladles and jellyspoons:
I come before you
To stand behind you
And tell you something
I know nothing about.

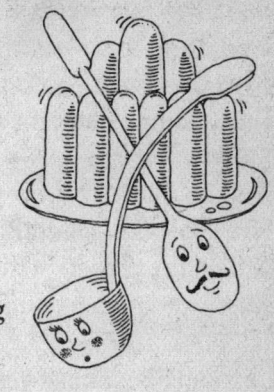

Next Thursday,
The day after Friday,
There'll be a ladies' meeting
For men only.

Wear your best clothes
If you haven't any,
And if you can come
Please stay home.

Admission is free,
You can pay at the door.
We'll give you a seat
So you can sit on the floor

It makes no difference
Where you sit;
The kid in the gallery
Is sure to spit.

UNKNOWN

Colonel Fazackerley

Colonel Fazackerly Butterworth-Toast
Bought an old castle complete with a ghost,
But someone or other forgot to declare
To Colonel Fazack that the spectre was there.

On the very first evening, while waiting to dine,
The Colonel was taking a fine sherry wine,
When the ghost, with a furious flash and a flare,
Shot out of the chimney and shivered, 'Beware!'

Colonel Fazackerley put down his glass
And said, 'My dear fellow, that's really first class!
I just can't conceive how you do it at all.
I imagine you're going to a Fancy Dress Ball?'

At this, the dread ghost gave a withering cry.
Said the Colonel (his monocle firm in his eye),
'Now just how you do it I wish I could think.
So sit down and tell me, and please have a drink.'

The ghost in his phosphorous cloak gave a roar
And floated about between ceiling and floor.
He walked through a wall and returned through a
    pane
And backed up the chimney and came down again.

Said the Colonel, 'With laughter I'm feeling quite
    weak!'
(As trickles of merriment ran down his cheek).

'My house-warming party I hope you won't spurn.
You *must* say you'll come and you'll give us a turn!'

At this, the poor spectre – quite out of his wits –
Proceeded to shake himself almost to bits.
He rattled his chains and he clattered his bones
And he filled the whole castle with mumbles and
   moans.

But Colonel Fazackerley, just as before,
Was simply delighted and called out, 'Encore!'
At which the ghost vanished, his efforts in vain,
And never was seen at the castle again.

'Oh dear, what a pity!' said Colonel Fazack.
'I don't know his name, so I can't call him back.'
And then with a smile that was hard to define,
Colonel Fazackerley went in to dine.

CHARLES CAUSLEY

What do ghosts eat for dinner?
Ghoulash.

Like a bird

There was an old man who averred
He had learned how to fly like a bird.
Cheered by thousands of people
He leapt from the steeple –
This tomb states the day it occurred.

UNKNOWN

What's small and feathery and goes putta-putta?

An outboard budgie.

A young fellow

There was a young fellow called Green
Whose musical sense was not keen,
He said: 'It's most odd,
But I cannot tell *God*
Save the Weasel from *Pop goes the Queen!*'

CAROLYN WELLS

The pessimist

Nothing to do but work,
Nothing to eat but food,
Nothing to wear but clothes,
To keep one from going nude.

Nothing to breathe but air,
  Quick as a flash 'tis gone;
Nowhere to fall but off,
  Nowhere to stand but on.

Nothing to comb but hair,
  Nowhere to sleep but in bed,
Nothing to weep but tears,
  Nothing to bury but dead.

Nothing to sing but songs,
  Ah, well, alas, alack!
Nowhere to go but out,
  Nowhere to come but back.

Nothing to see but sights,
  Nothing to quench but thirst,
Nothing to have but what we've got.
  Thus through life we are cursed.

Nothing to strike but a gait;
  Everything moves that goes.
Nothing at all but common sense
  Can ever withstand these woes.

BENJAMIN FRANKLIN KING

What is round and bad-tempered?

A vicious circle.

The new vestments

There lived an old man in The kingdom of Tess,
Who invented a purely original dress;
And when it was perfectly made and complete,
He opened the door, and walked into the street.
By way of a hat, he'd a loaf of Brown Bread,
In the middle of which he inserted his head; –
His Shirt was made up of no end of dead Mice,
The warmth of whose skins was quite fluffy and
  nice; –
His Drawers were of Rabbit-skins; – so were his
  Shoes; –
His Stockings were skins, – but it is not known
  whose; –
His Waistcoat and Trowsers were made of Pork
  Chops; –
His Buttons were Jujubes and Chocolate Drops; –
His Coat was all Pancakes with Jam for a border,
And a girdle of Biscuits to keep it in order;
And he wore over all, as a screen from bad weather,
A Cloak of green Cabbage-leaves stitched all
  together.

He had walked a short way, when he heard a great
  noise,
Of all sorts of Beasticles, Birdlings and Boys; –
And from every long street and dark lane in the
  town
Beasts, Birdles, and Boys in a tumult rushed down.

Two Cows and a half ate his Cabbage-leaf Cloak; –
Four Apes seized his Girdle, which vanished like
    smoke; –
Three Kids ate up half of his Pancaky Coat, –
And the tails were devour'd by an ancient He
    Goat; –
An army of Dogs in a twinkling tore *up* his
Pork Waistcoat and Trowsers to give to their
    Puppies; –
And while they were growling, and mumbling the
    Chops,
Ten Boys prigged the Jujubes and Chocolate
    Drops. –

He tried to run back to his house, but in vain,
For Scores of fat Pigs came again and again; –
They rushed out of stables and hovels and doors, –
They tore off his stockings, his shoes, and his
    drawers; –

And now from the housetops with screechings descend,
Striped, spotted, white, black, and grey Cats without end,
They jumped on his shoulders and knocked off his hat, –
When Crows, Ducks, and Hens made a mincemeat of that; –
They speedily flew at his sleeves in a trice,
And utterly tore up his Shirt of dead Mice; –
They swallowed the last of his Shirt with a squall, –
Whereon he ran home with no clothes on at all.
And he said to himself as he bolted the door,
'I will not wear a similar dress any more,
'Any more, any more, any more, never more!'

EDWARD LEAR

What is a caterpillar?
A worm in a fur coat.

What's black and white and noisy?
A zebra with a drum set.

What did the mouse say when it broke its front tooth?
Hard cheese.

50

There was an old woman

There was an old woman who swallowed a fly;
I wonder why
She swallowed a fly.
Poor old woman, she's sure to die.

There was an old woman who swallowed a spider;
That wriggled and jiggled and wriggled inside her;
She swallowed the spider to catch the fly,
I wonder why
She swallowed a fly.
Poor old woman, she's sure to die.

There was an old woman who swallowed a bird;
How absurd
To swallow a bird.
She swallowed the bird to catch the spider,
That wriggled and jiggled and wriggled inside her.
She swallowed the spider to catch the fly,
I wonder why
She swallowed a fly.
Poor old woman, she's sure to die.

There was an old woman who swallowed a dog;
She went the whole hog
And swallowed a dog;
She swallowed the dog to catch the cat,
She swallowed the cat to catch the bird,

She swallowed the bird to catch the spider,
That wriggled and jiggled and wriggled inside her.
She swallowed the spider to catch the fly,
I wonder why
She swallowed a fly.
Poor old woman, she's sure to die.

There·was an old woman who swallowed a cow;
I wonder how
She swallowed a cow;
She swallowed the cow to catch the dog,
She swallowed the dog to catch the cat,
She swallowed the cat to catch the bird,
She swallowed the bird to catch the spider,
That wriggled and jiggled and wriggled inside her.
She swallowed the spider to catch the fly,
I wonder why
She swallowed a fly.
Poor old woman, she's sure to die.

There was an old woman who swallowed a horse;
She died of course!

TRADITIONAL

CUSTOMER: *I found a fly in one of those currant buns I bought yesterday.*

SHOP ASSISTANT: *Bring it back and I'll exchange it for a currant.*

The old sailor

There was once an old sailor my grandfather knew
Who had so many things which he wanted to do
That, whenever he thought it was time to begin,
He couldn't because of the state he was in.

He was shipwrecked, and lived on an island for
    weeks,
And he wanted a hat, and he wanted some breeks;
And he wanted some nets, or a line and some
    hooks
For the turtles and things which you read of in
    books.

And, thinking of this, he remembered a thing
Which he wanted (for water) and that was a spring;
And he thought that to talk to he'd look for, and
    keep
(If he found it), a goat, or some chickens and sheep.

Then, because of the weather, he wanted a hut
With a door (to come in by) which opened and
    shut
(With a jerk, which was useful if snakes were
    about),
And a very strong lock to keep savages out.

He began on the fish-hooks, and when he'd begun
He decided he couldn't because of the sun.

So he knew what he ought to begin with, and that
Was to find, or to make, a large sun-stopping hat.

He was making the hat with some leaves from a
    tree,
When he thought, 'I'm as hot as a body can be,
And I've nothing to take for my terrible thirst;
So I'll look for a spring, and I'll look for it first.'

Then he thought as he started, 'Oh, dear and oh,
    dear!
I'll be lonely tomorrow with nobody here!'
So he made in his note-book a couple of notes:
'I must first find some chickens' and 'No, I mean
    goats.'

He had just seen a goat (which he knew by the
 shape)
When he thought, 'But I must have a boat for
 escape.
But a boat means a sail, which means needles and
 thread;
So I'd better sit down and make needles instead.'

He began on a needle, but thought as he worked,
That, if this was an island where savages lurked,
Sitting safe in his hut he'd have nothing to fear,
Whereas now they might suddenly breathe in his
 ear!

So he thought of his hut . . . and he thought of his
 boat,
Of his hat and his breeks, and his chickens and
 goat,
And the hooks (for his food) and the spring
 (for his thirst)
But he never could think which he ought to do
 first.

And so in the end he did nothing at all,
But basked on the shingle wrapped up in a shawl.
And I think it was dreadful the way he behaved –
He did nothing but basking until he was saved!

A. A. MILNE

What does the sea say to the sand?

Nothing. It just waves.

Smiling villain

Forth from his den to steal he stole,
His bags of chink he chunk,
And many a wicked smile he smole,
And many a wink he wunk.

UNKNOWN

The sniffle

In spite of her sniffle,
Isabel's chiffle.
Some girls with a sniffle
Would be weepy and tiffle;
They would look awful,
Like a rained-on waffle,
But Isabel's chiffle
In spite of her sniffle.
Her nose is more red
With a cold in her head,
But then, to be sure,
Her eyes are bluer.
Some girls with a snuffle,
Their tempers are uffle,
But when Isabel's snivelly
She's snivelly civilly,
And when she is snuffly
She's perfectly luffly.

OGDEN NASH

A bird in the hand makes it difficult to wipe your nose.

The lesson

A poem that raises the question:
Should there be capital punishment in schools?

Chaos ruled OK in the classroom
as bravely the teacher walked in
the havocwreakers ignored him
his voice was lost in the din

'The theme for today is violence
and homework will be set
I'm going to teach you a lesson
one that you'll never forget.'

He picked on a boy who was shouting
and throttled him then and there
then garotted the girl behind him
(the one with grotty hair) —

Then sword in hand he hacked his way
between the chattering rows
'First come first severed' he declared
'fingers, feet or toes.'

He threw the sword at a latecomer
it struck with deadly aim
then pulling out a shotgun
he continued with his game

The first blast cleared the back row
(where those who skive hang out)
they collapsed like rubber dinghies
when the plugs are pulled out

'Please may I leave the room sir?'
a trembling vandal enquired
'Of course you may' said teacher
put the gun to his temple and fired

The Head popped a head round the door
to see why a din was being made
nodding understandingly
then tossed in a grenade

And when the ammo was well spent
with blood on every chair
Silence shuffled forward
with its hands up in the air

The teacher surveyed the carnage
the dying and the dead
He waggled a finger severely
'now let that be a lesson' he said

ROGER McGOUGH

A caution to everybody

Consider the auk;
Becoming extinct because he forgot how to fly, and
    could only walk.
Consider man, who may well become extinct
Because he forgot how to walk and learned how to
    fly before he thinked.

OGDEN NASH

He thought he saw

He thought he saw a Buffalo
Upon the chimney piece:
He looked again, and found it was
His Sister's Husband's Niece.
'Unless you leave this house!' he said,
'I'll send for the police!'

He thought he saw a Rattlesnake
That questioned him in Greek:
He looked again and found it was
The Middle of Next Week.
'The one thing I regret,' he said,
'Is that it cannot speak!'

He thought he saw a Banker's Clerk
Descending from the bus:
He looked again, and found it was
A Hippopotamus.
'If this should stay to dine,' he said,
'There won't be much for us!'

PAY
AS YOU
ENTER

He thought he saw a Kangaroo
That worked a coffee mill:
He looked again, and found it was
A Vegetable-Pill.
'Were I to swallow this,' he said,
'I should be very ill!'

He thought he saw
  a Coach-and-Four
That stood beside his bed:
He looked again, and found it was
A Bear without a Head.
'Poor thing,' he said,
  'poor silly thing!
'It's waiting to be fed!'

He thought he saw an Albatross
That fluttered round the lamp:
He looked again, and found it was
A Penny-Postage-Stamp.
'You'd best be getting home,' he said:
'The nights are very damp!'

LEWIS CARROLL

A man sat up all night wondering where the sun had gone.

Next morning it dawned on him.

One old ox

One old ox opening oysters,
Two toads totally tired
Trying to trot to Tewkesbury,
Three tame tigers taking tea,
Four fat friars fishing for frogs,
Five fairies finding fire-flies,
Six soldiers shooting snipe,
Seven salmon sailing in the Solway,
Eight elegant engineers eating excellent eggs;
Nine nimble noblemen nibbling nine-pins,
Ten tall tinkers tasting tamarinds,
Eleven electors eating early endive,
Twelve tremendous tale-bearers telling truth.

UNKNOWN

Jabberwocky

'Twas brillig, and the slithy toves
   Did gyre and gimble in the wabe;
All mimsy were the borogoves,
   And the mome raths outgrabe.

'Beware the Jabberwock, my son!
   The jaws that bite, the claws that catch!
Beware the Jubjub bird, and shun
   The frumious Bandersnatch!'

He took his vorpal sword in hand:
   Long time the manxome foe he sought –
So rested he by the Tumtum tree,
   And stood awhile in thought.

And as in uffish thought he stood,
   The Jabberwock, with eyes of flame,
Came whiffling through the tulgey wood,
   And burbled as it came!

One, two! One, two! And through and through
  The vorpal blade went snicker-snack!
He left it dead, and with its head
  He went galumphing back.

'And hast thou slain the Jabberwock?
  Come to my arms, my beamish boy!
O frabjous day! Callooh! Callay!'
  He chortled in his joy.

'Twas brillig, and the slithy toves
  Did gyre and gimble in the wabe;
All mimsy were the borogoves,
  And the mome raths outgrabe.

LEWIS CARROLL

Two cats of Kilkenny

There once were two cats of Kilkenny,
Each thought there was one cat too many;
So they fought and they fit,
And they scratched and they bit,
Till, excepting their nails
And the tips of their tails,
Instead of two cats, there weren't any.

UNKNOWN

What happened to the cat that swallowed a ball of wool?

She had mittens.

What am I?

Four stiff-standers,
Four lily-landers,
Two lookers, two crookers,
And a wig-wag.

The purple cow

I never Saw a Purple Cow,
I never Hope to See One;
But I can Tell you, Anyhow,
I'd rather See than Be One.

GELETT BURGESS

What do you get if you cross a cow, a sheep and a goat?

The milky bar kid.

What do you get if you cross a sheep and a kangaroo?

A woolly jumper.

The centipede

The Centipede was happy quite,
Until the Toad in fun
Said 'Pray which leg goes after which?'

And worked her mind to such a pitch,
She lay distracted in the ditch
Considering how to run.

MRS EDMUND CRASTER

What goes '99-bump-99-bump'?
A centipede with a wooden leg.

The Snitterjipe

In mellow orchards, rich and ripe,
Is found the luminous Snitterjipe.
Bad boys who climb the bulging trees
Feel his sharp breath about their knees;
His trembling whiskers tickle so,
They squeak and squeal till they let go.
They hear his far-from-friendly bark;
They see his eyeballs in the dark
Shining and shifting in their sockets
As round and big as pears in pockets.
They feel his hot and wrinkly hide;
They see his nostrils flaming wide,
His tapering teeth, his jutting jaws,
His tongue, his tail, his twenty claws.
His hairy shadow in the moon,
It makes them sweat, it makes them swoon;
And as they climb the orchard wall,
They let their pilfered pippins fall.
The Snitterjipe suspends pursuit
And falls upon the fallen fruit;
And while they flee the monster fierce,
Apples, not boys, his talons pierce.
With thumping hearts they hear him munch –
Six apples at a time he'll crunch.

At length he falls asleep, and they
On tiptoe take their homeward way.
But long before the blackbirds pipe
To welcome day, the Snitterjipe
Has fled afar, and on the green
Only his fearsome prints are seen.

JAMES REEVES

The serpent

There was a Serpent who had to sing.
There was. There was.
He simply gave up Serpenting.
Because. Because.

He didn't like his Kind of Life;
He couldn't find a proper Wife;
He was a Serpent with a soul;
He got no Pleasure down his Hole.
And so, of course, he had to Sing,
And Sing he did, like Anything!
The Birds, they were, they were Astounded;
And various Measures Propounded
To stop the Serpent's Awful Racket:
They bought a Drum. He wouldn't Whack it.
They sent – you always send – to Cuba
And got a Most Commodious Tuba;

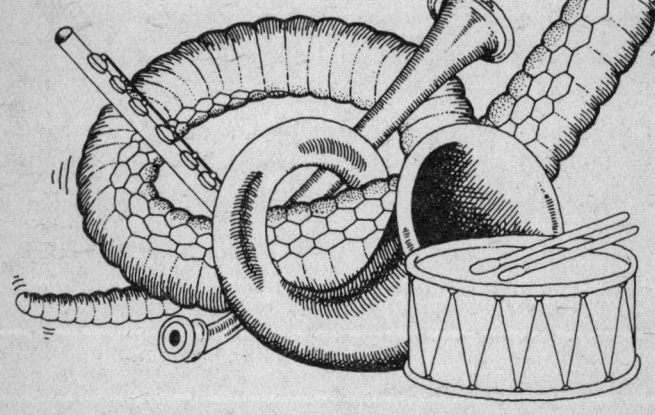

They got a Horn, they got a Flute,
But Nothing would suit.
He said, 'Look, Birds, all this is futile:
I do *not* like to Bang or Tootle.'
And then he cut loose with a Horrible Note
That practically split the Top of his Throat.
'You see,' he said, with a Serpent's Leer,
'I'm serious about my Singing Career!'
And the Woods Resounded with many a Shriek
As the Birds flew off to the End of Next Week.

THEODORE ROETHKE

What did the python say to his victim?

'I've got a crush on you.'

The camp follower

There's a long, long worm a-crawling
Across the roof of my tent.
I can hear the whistle calling,
And it's time I went.
There's the cold, cold water waiting
For me to take my morning dip.
And when I return
I'll find that worm
Upon my pillow-slip.

UNKNOWN

What's green and dangerous?

A caterpillar with a machine gun.

What a wonderful bird

What a wonderful bird the frog are!
When he stand he sit almost;
When he hop he fly almost.
He ain't got no sense hardly;
He ain't got no tail hardly either.

When he sit, he sit on what he ain't got almost.

UNKNOWN

At the zoo

First I saw the white bear, then I saw the black;
Then I saw the camel with a hump upon its back;
Then I saw the grey wolf, with mutton in his maw;
Then I saw the wombat waddle on the straw;
Then I saw the elephant a-waving of his trunk;
Then I saw the monkeys – mercy, how unpleasantly
   they smelt!

WILLIAM MAKEPEACE THACKERAY

What's black, red and white?

A baby skunk with nappy rash.

The elephant

When people call this beast to mind,
They marvel more and more
At such a *little* tail behind,
So LARGE a trunk before.

HILAIRE BELLOC

Why do elephants wear green felt hats?

So they can walk across billiard tables without being seen.

The camel's complaint

Canary-birds feed on sugar and seed,
    Parrots have crackers to crunch;
And as for the poodles, they tell me the noodles
    Have chicken and cream for their lunch.
      But there's never a question
      About *my* digestion –
        Anything does for me.

Cats, you're aware, can repose in a chair,
    Chickens can roost upon rails;
Puppies are able to sleep in a stable,
    And oysters can slumber in pails.
      But no one supposes
      A poor camel dozes –
        Any place does for me.

Lambs are enclosed where it's never exposed,
  Coops are constructed for hens;
Kittens are treated to houses well heated,
  And pigs are protected by pens.
    But a camel comes handy
    Wherever its sandy –
      Anywhere does for me.

People would laugh if you rode a giraffe,
  Or mounted the back of an ox;
It's nobody's habit to ride on a rabbit,
  Or try to bestraddle a fox.
    But as for a camel, he's
    Ridden by families –
      Any *load* does for me.

A snake is as round as a hole in the ground,
  And weasels are wavy and sleek;
And no alligator would ever be straighter
  Than lizards that live in a creek.
    But a camel's all lumpy
    And bumpy and humpy –
      Any *shape* does for me.

CHARLES E. CARRYL

The centipede song

'I've eaten many strange and scrumptious dishes in
   my time,
Like jellied gnats and dandyprats and earwigs
   cooked in slime,
And mice with rice – they're really nice
When roasted in their prime.
(But don't forget to sprinkle them with just a pinch
   of grime.)

'I've eaten fresh mudburgers by the greatest cooks
   there are,
And scrambled dregs and stinkbugs' eggs and
   hornets stewed in tar,
And pails of snails and lizards' tails,
And beetles by the jar.
(A beetle is improved by just a splash of vinegar.)

'I often eat boiled slobbages. They're grand when
   served beside
Minced doodlebugs and curried slugs. And have
   you ever tried
Mosquitoes' toes and wampfish roes
Most delicately fried?
(The only trouble is they disagree with my inside.)

'I'm mad for crispy wasp-stings on a piece of
   buttered toast,
And pickled spines of porcupines. And then a
   gorgeous roast

Of dragon's flesh, well hung, not fresh –
It costs a pound at most,
(And comes to you in barrels if you order it by
    post.)

'I crave the tasty tentacles of octopi for tea
I like hot-dogs, I LOVE hot-frogs, and surely you'll
    agree
A plate of soil with engine oil's
A super recipe.
(I hardly need to mention that it's practically free.)

'For dinner on my birthday shall I tell you what I
    chose:
Hot noodles made from poodles on a slice of
    garden hose –
And a rather smelly jelly
Made of armadillo's toes.
(The jelly is delicious, but you have to hold your
    nose.)

'Now comes,' *the Centipede delared*, 'the burden of
    my speech:
These foods are rare beyond compare – some are
    right out of reach;
But there's no doubt I'd go without
A million plates of each
For one small mite,
One tiny bite
Of this FANTASTIC PEACH!'

ROALD DAHL

The giraffe

You must not chaff
The tall Giraffe
About his size of collars,
Nor watch him drink,
And rudely wink
And ask him how he swallers.

When at the Zoo
It will not do
To criticize his spots,
Nor ask him when
You pass his pen
To tie his neck in knots.

Nor is it nice
To give advice
On troubles of the spine –
The tall Giraffe
Enjoys a laugh,
But there he draws the line.

JOHN JOY BELL

What is the highest form of animal life?
A giraffe.

76

On the death of a giraffe

They say, God wot!
She died upon the spot:
But then in spots she was so rich –
I wonder which?

THOMAS HOOD

Silly old baboon

There was a Baboon
Who, one afternoon,
Said, 'I think I will fly to the sun.'
So, with two great palms
Strapped to his arms,
He started his take-off run.

Mile after mile
He galloped in style
But never once left the ground.
'You're running too slow,'
Said a passing crow,
'Try reaching the speed of sound.'

So he put on a spurt –
By God how it hurt!
The soles of his feet caught fire.
There were great clouds of steam
As he raced through a stream
But he still didn't get any higher.

Racing on through the night,
Both his knees caught alight
And smoke billowed out from his rear.
Quick to his aid
Came a fire brigade
Who chased him for over a year.

Many moons passed by.
Did Baboons ever fly?
Did he ever get to the sun?
I've just heard today
That he's well on his way!
He'll be passing through Acton at one.

P.S. Well, what do you expect from a Baboon?

SPIKE MILLIGAN

How do you catch a monkey?

*Hang upside-down in a tree and make a noise like a
banana.*

The rabbit

The Rabbit has an evil mind,
Although he looks so good and kind.

His life is a complete disgrace
Although he has so soft a face.

I hardly like to let you know
How far his wickedness will go.

Enough, if this poor rhyme declares
His fearful cruelty to hares.
He does his very best to keep
These gentle animals from sleep,

By joining in with noisy throngs
Of rabbits singing ribald songs.
To wake their fears and make them bound,
He simulates the Basset-hound.

And if he meets them after dark,
He imitates the greyhound's bark.

LORD ALFRED DOUGLAS

What do you get when you pour hot water down a rabbit-hole?

A hot cross bunny.

I bought me a cat

I bought me a cat, my cat pleased me
I fed my cat under yonder tree
My cat says 'Fiddle eye fee.'

I bought me a duck, my duck pleased me
I fed my duck under yonder tree
My duck says 'Quaa, quaa'
My cat says 'Fiddle eye fee'.

I bought me a goose, my goose pleased me
I fed my goose under yonder tree
My goose says 'Quaw, quaw'
My duck says 'Quaa, quaa'
My cat says 'Fiddle eye fee'.

I bought me a hen, my hen pleased me
I fed my hen under yonder tree
My hen says 'Shimmy shack, shimmy shack'
My goose says 'Quaw, quaw'
My duck says 'Quaa, quaa'
My cat says 'Fiddle eye fee'.

I bought me a pig, my pig pleased me
I fed my pig under yonder tree
My pig says 'Griffey, griffey'
My hen says 'Shimmy shack, shimmy shack'
My goose says 'Quaw, quaw'
My duck says 'Quaa, quaa'
My cat says 'Fiddle eye fee'.

I bought me a cow, my cow pleased me
I fed my cow under yonder tree
My cow says, 'Baw, baw'
My pig says 'Griffey, griffey'
My hen says 'Shimmy shack, shimmy shack'
My goose says 'Quaw, quaw'
My duck says 'Quaa, quaa'
My cat says 'Fiddle eye fee'.

I bought me a horse, my horse pleased me
I fed my horse under yonder tree
My horse says 'Neigh, neigh'
My cow says 'Baw, baw'
My pig says 'Griffey, griffey'
My hen says 'Shimmy shack, shimmy shack'
My goose says 'Quaw, quaw'
My duck says 'Quaa, quaa'
My cat says 'Fiddle eye fee'.

I bought me a wife, my wife pleased me
I fed my wife under yonder tree
My wife says 'Honey, honey'
My horse says 'Neigh, neigh'
My cow says 'Baw, baw'
My pig says 'Griffey, griffey'
My hen says 'Shimmy shack, shimmy shack'
My goose says 'Quaw, quaw'
My duck says 'Quaa, quaa'
My cat says 'Fiddle eye fee'.

TRADITIONAL AMERICAN

What do we call a cat that swallows a duck?

A duck-filled-fatty-puss.

The shark

A treacherous monster is the Shark
He never makes the least remark.

And when he sees you on the sand,
He doesn't seem to want to land.

He watches you take off your clothes,
And not the least excitement shows.

His eyes do not grow bright or roll,
He has astounding self-control.

He waits till you are quite undrest,
And seems to take no interest.

And when towards the sea you leap,
He looks as if he were asleep.

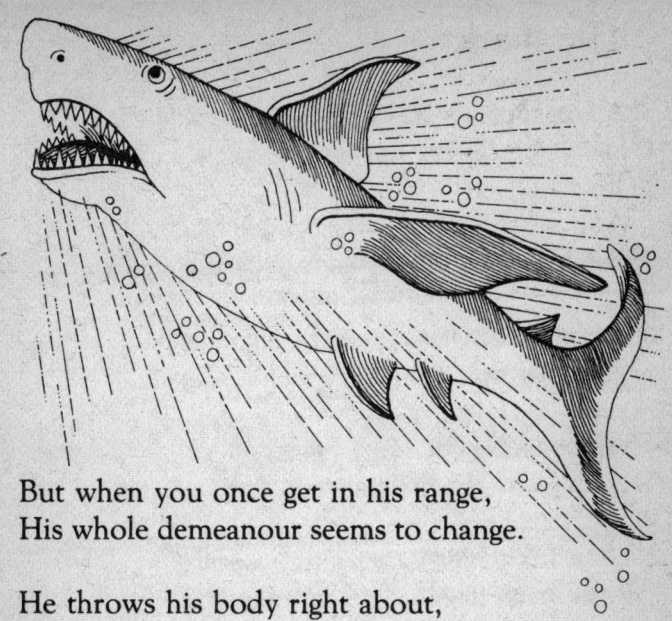

But when you once get in his range,
His whole demeanour seems to change.

He throws his body right about,
And his true character comes out.

It's no use crying or appealing,
He seems to lose all decent feeling.

After this warning you will wish
To keep clear of this treacherous fish.
His back is black, his stomach white,
He has a very dangerous bite.

LORD ALFRED DOUGLAS

What shivers and lies at the bottom of the sea?

A nervous wreck.

Hard cheese

The grown-ups are all safe,
Tucked up inside,
Where they belong.

They doze into the telly,
Bustle through the washing-up,
Snore into the fire,
Rustle through the paper.

They're all there,
Out of harm's way.

Now it's *our* street:
All the back-yards,
All the gardens,
All the shadows,
All the dark corners,
All the privet-hedges,
All the lamp-posts,
All the door-ways.

Here is an important announcement:
The army of occupation
Is confined to barracks.
Hooray.

We're the natives.
We creep out at night,

Play everywhere,
Swing on *all* the lamp-posts,
Slit your gizzard?

Then about nine o'clock,
They send out search-parties.

We can hear them coming.
And we crouch
In the garden-sheds,
Behind the dust-bins,
Up the alley-ways,
Inside the dust-bins,
Or stand stock-still,
And pull ourselves in,
As thin as a pin,
Behind the lamp-posts.

And they stand still,
And peer into the dark.
They take a deep breath –
You can hear it for miles –
And, then, they bawl,
They shout, they caterwaul:
'J-i-i-i-i-i-mmeeee!'
'Timeforbed. D'youhearme?'
'M-a-a-a-a-a-reeee!'
'J-o-o-o-o-o-hnneeee!'
'S-a-a-a-a-a-mmeeee!'
'Mary!' 'Jimmy!'
'Johnny!' 'Sammy!'
Like cats. With very big mouths.

Then we give ourselves up,
Prisoners-of-war.
Till tomorrow night.

But just you wait.
One of these nights
We'll hold out,
We'll lie doggo,
And wait, and wait,
Till they just give up
And mumble
And go to bed.
You just wait.
They'll see!

JUSTIN ST JOHN

The Derby ram

As I was going to Derby, sir,
Upon a market day,
I saw the biggest ram, sir,
That ever was fed on hay.

And indeed, sir, 'tis true, sir,
I never was given to lie
And if you'd been to Derby, sir,
You'd have seen him as well as I.

This ram was fat behind, sir,
This ram was fat before.
He measured ten yards round, sir,
If not a little more.

He had four feet to walk on, sir,
He had four feet to stand,
And every foot he had, sir,
Did cover an acre of land.

The man who killed this ram, sir,
Was drowned in all the blood,
And he who held the dish, sir,
Was carried away in the flood.

The mutton that ram made, sir,
Gave all the Army meat,
And what was left, I'm told, sir,
Was served out to the Fleet.

The wool grew on his back, sir,
It reached up to the sky,
And there the eagles built their nests,
I heard the young ones cry.

The wool grew on his belly, sir,
It reached down to the ground,
And that was sold in Derby town
For forty thousand pound.

The horns upon this ram, sir,
They reached up to the moon.
A little boy went up in January
And he never got back till June.

And all the boys of Derby
Came begging for his eyes,
To make themselves some footballs,
For they were of football size.

TRADITIONAL

The computer's first Christmas card

Jolly merry
holly berry
jolly berry
merry holly
happy jolly
jolly jelly
jelly belly
bellymerry
holly heppy
jolly Molly
marry Jerry

EDWIN MORGAN

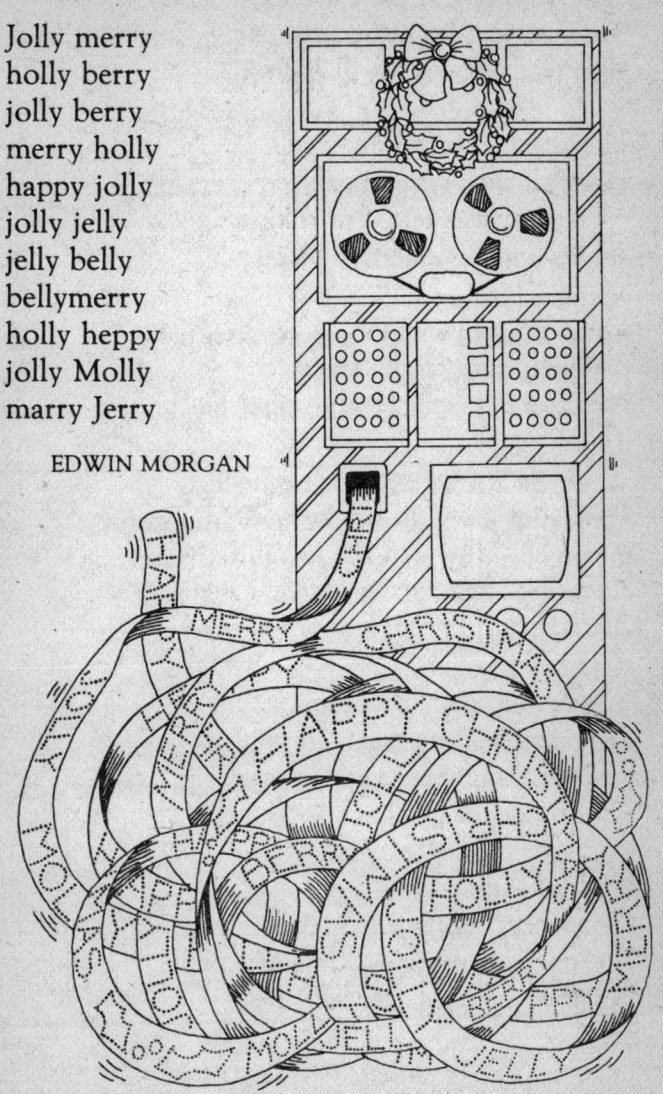

Old zip coon

There was a man who could execute
Old Zip Coon on his yellow flute,
But he couldn't make a penny with his
TOOTLE-TI-TOOT,
TOOTLE-OOTLE-OOTLE TOOTLE-TI-TOOT.

One day he met with a singular,
Quaint old man with a big tuba,
But he couldn't make a penny with his
UM-PA-PA,
TOOTLE-OOTLE-OOTLE, UM-PA-PA.

They met a man who was travelling
With a big bass drum and a cymbal thing,
But he couldn't make a penny with his
BOOM-ZING-ZING.
TOOTLE-OOTLE, UM-PA, BOOM-ZING-ZING.

The man with the flute went TOOTLE-TI-TOOT,
And the other man he went UM-PA,
And the man with the drum and the cymbal
thing
Went BOOM-BOOMPETY-BOOM-BOOM,
ZING-ZING,
And oh, the pennies that the people fling,
When they hear the TOOTLE, UM-PA,
BOOM-ZING-ZING

BOOM-ZING, BOOM-ZING, BOOM-ZING-ZING,
TOOTLE-OOTLE, UM-PA, BOOM-ZING-ZING.

UNKNOWN

Next!

I thought that I would like to see
The early world that used to be,
That mastadonic mausoleum,
The Natural History Museum.
At midnight in the vasty hall
The fossils gathered for a ball.
High above notices and bulletins
Loomed up the Mesozoic skeletons.
Aroused by who knows what elixirs,
They ground along like concrete mixers.
They bowed and scraped in reptile pleasure,
And then began to tread the measure.
There were no drums or saxophones,
But just the clatter of their bones,
A rolling, rattling carefree circus
Of mammoth polkas and mazurkas.
Pterodactyls and brontosauruses
Sang ghostly prehistoric choruses.
Amid the megalosauric wassail
I caught the eye of one small fossil.
Cheer up, old man he said, and winked –
It's kind of fun to be extinct.

OGDEN NASH

Index of authors

Index of first lines